NOMO

THE TORNADO WHO TOOK AMERICA BY STORM

By Edmon J. Rodman

Lowell House
Juvenile
Los Angeles

CONTEMPORARY BOOKS
Chicago

Publisher: Jack Artenstein
Vice President/General Manager, Juvenile Division: Elizabeth D. Amos
Director of Publishing Services: Rena Copperman
Project Editor: Michael Artenstein
Managing Editor: Jessica Oifer
Art Director: Lisa-Theresa Lenthall
Designer: Carolyn Wendt

Library of Congress Catalog Card Number is available.

ISBN: 1-56565-394-7

Manufactured in the United States of America

10 9 8 7 6 5 4 3 2 1

Lowell House books can be purchased at special discounts
when ordered in bulk for premiums and special sales.
Contact Department JH at the following address:

Lowell House Juvenile
2029 Century Park East, Suite 3290
Los Angeles, CA 90067

*This book is dedicated to parents everywhere
who play catch with their kids, and
to my kids, Elan, Benzi, and Micah.*

ACKNOWLEDGMENTS

Many thanks to the people who made this book possible: the staff at Lowell House, including Michael Artenstein, Jessica Oifer, and Rena Copperman; copy editor David Griffith; interviewer/interpreter Yuko Miura; John A. Olguin, archivist for the Los Angeles Dodgers; Jim Moorehead, media relations manager for the San Francisco Giants; Shirley Ito and Michael Salmon, librarians at Ziffren Center Library; Larry Fuhrmann; Koichi Ono; Robert Klevens; and Jim Nishi of the *Daily Yomiuri.*

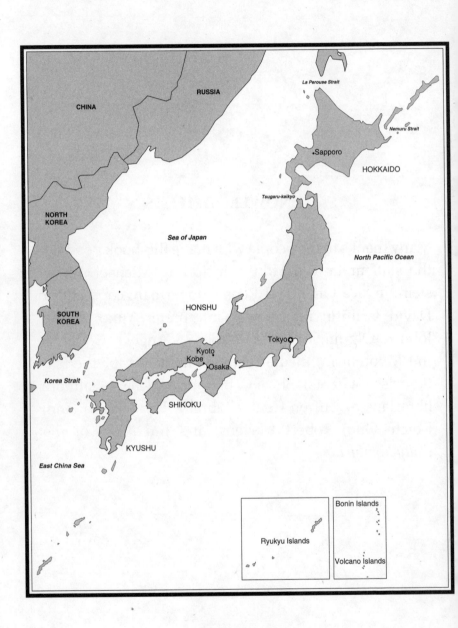

JAPAN

Ishi no ue ni mo san nen

Patience and perseverance will
wear out even a stone.

CONTENTS

INTRODUCTION

"**W**hat do you know about Hideo Nomo?" the voice on the other end of the phone asked. It was a warm day in June 1995 when I received this call from an editor at the RGA Publishing Group, Inc. I had to think for a moment—hmm . . . Hideo Nomo. He was a pitcher, I knew that much. I also knew that he was playing for the Los Angeles Dodgers and evidently he was doing quite well. But that was about it.

We discussed in particular the special opportunities that a book on Hideo Nomo would present. Not only is Nomo an exceptional athlete, he is also a *Japanese* athlete playing in America. His fascinating story would allow us to present readers with various aspects of Japanese life, including comparisons between Japan and the United States. Of course, we would also talk about baseball—fastballs and forkballs, strikeout records, and pennant races.

I have eaten my share of Japanese food. I've even amused my wife with my feeble efforts at ordering meals in Japanese. But if truth be told, researching this book was my first real introduction to all things Japanese. The editor on the project, Michael Artenstein, speaks and writes Japanese. He tutored me on some of the basic greetings we all agreed would be necessary in the course of my many interviews for the book. Yuko Miura was brought in on the project as an interpreter/translator. She conducted several key interviews, including one with Hideo Nomo's father, Shizuo.

Then, shortly after the 1995 Major League All-Star Game—in which Nomo was the National League's starting pitcher—I set to work on the book. One of the first things I discovered was that both baseball-loving countries—Japan and America—are well connected by phones, faxes, modems, and fans. While Americans were watching Nomo as the sun vanished beyond the horizon, baseball fans in Japan were watching him as it rose. I learned that the Baseball Hall of Fame in Cooperstown, New York, is not the only hall of fame—there is one in Japan as well. It soon became evident to me that Americans are not the only fans who love to read box scores or chant a star player's name as he walks onto the field. They do these things in Japan, too.

I also discovered in my research there are Americans

who have emigrated to Japan who are very active in baseball there. I had heard of some American ballplayers going over to Japan to play ball. But I never knew they were followed by other Americans—writers and journalists, among others.

Hideo Nomo's rise in Japanese baseball came about after much dedication and perseverance. His success on two continents makes him truly extraordinary. But this superstar is a real person, like you or me, with disappointments, setbacks, and challenges that at one time seemed insurmountable.

I discovered that Nomo's dream to play in America was not the only dream in the story. Dodger President Peter O'Malley also had a dream: to internationalize baseball by bringing over players from around the world. Between the coming together of these two dreams, you will discover a mosaic of coaches, agents, contracts, and an international search for excellence in baseball.

You will also find that this is not the story of a man who desired stardom. In fact, off the playing field, both here and in Japan, Nomo has done almost everything in his power to avoid the bright lights of fame.

Nomo's whirlwind rookie season in the major leagues has caught everyone by surprise. And because of his success, Americans will never look at Japanese athletes quite the same way. Nomo has proved himself. He has proved that Japanese baseball, which has always been regarded as inferior to the brand of baseball played here, might just be different. Nomo's arrival in America has also provided both countries the perfect opportunity for cultural exchange and the means to a better understanding. We are two vastly different nations who now share a common hero.

—E.J.R.

CHAPTER I

A Midsummer's Dream

On a hot night in Arlington, Texas, Hideo Nomo stands on the pitching mound. He toes the pitching rubber and looks toward his catcher for the sign. Nomo is pitching in the 66th Annual Major League All-Star Game, and just being here on this raised dirt is a chance of a lifetime for the young pitcher. It's the bottom of the first inning, and he's about to do what he's always dreamed of doing. He's about to match his skills against the best hitters in the world.

Hideo Nomo (pronounced Hee-deh-oh Noh-moh) is a twenty-six-year-old rookie pitcher from Japan. He throws blazing fastballs and wicked forkballs. He possesses a whirling windup, which, in Japan, has earned him the nickname "Tornado." He has come a long way to fulfill his dream of pitching against the world's best hitters. And tonight, Nomo will make history by becoming the first Japanese to play in a major league All-Star game.

His dream has become a reality.

Nomo looks cool on the mound. He doesn't want anyone to know how nervous he is. But he *is* nervous. More than 50,000 fans are watching his every move from the nearby stadium stands—American League fans, for the most part. They've come to this stadium, The Ballpark at Arlington, to watch the American League All-Star team defeat Nomo's National League All-Stars. After all, their hometown team, the Texas Rangers, is in the American League.

The crowd is noisy, and they're cheering hard for the other team. But that's not what's making Nomo nervous. The real tension is coming from another audience watching this All-Star game. It's coming from fans far from this spanking new ballpark.

More than 8,000 miles away in Tokyo, Japan, it's the middle of the morning, and on a normal day people would be at work and at school. But this morning, many people are not working. Thousands have gathered in the streets before giant TV screens; others sit in family rooms and offices across this island nation. All are watching their native son step up on the mound in Texas to pitch against baseball's best hitters.

It's been a difficult year for the Japanese. In January, more than 5,000 people perished in a devastating earthquake in Kobe, a port city not far from where Nomo grew up in Osaka. Nomo's unexpected success in America over the past few months has given the Japanese people something positive to think about in the aftermath of the deadly quake.

Nomo carries the weight of an entire country on his shoulders. If his pitches are hammered by the American batters, he will be a disappointment to Japanese baseball and to Japan. If he succeeds, the Japanese fans will rejoice.

The first game of baseball on record in America took place in 1846, in Hoboken, New Jersey. Twenty-seven years later in 1873, teacher Horace Wilson introduced the sport to Japan. Interestingly, Wilson's students played the game wearing wooden clogs called *geta*.

Nomo can't think about all that right now. Thinking about it makes him sweat. It makes him sweat even more than the 96 degree heat of this July 11 night. The American League pitcher kept Nomo's team from scoring in the top of the first inning. Nomo's job is to do the same to the American League hitters. It won't be easy.

Standing at the plate is the most dangerous leadoff

hitter in baseball, Kenny Lofton of the Cleveland Indians. Nomo and his catcher, Los Angeles Dodger teammate Mike Piazza, know they must get Lofton out. If the speedy center fielder reaches first base safely, he will probably steal second. Then perhaps third. On third base, a player as fast as Lofton can easily score on a hit, a fly ball, a wild pitch, even a groundout. If Lofton scores, it will be the start of a big inning for the American League. And that's the last thing Nomo and Piazza want.

The capacity crowd quiets down, focusing their attention on Nomo. They've been reading about him in the sports pages; they've seen his image on the nightly TV sports shows. But few have any knowledge of the obstacles he has had to overcome to make it to this historic night. His are the trials that face all men and women who undertake extraordinary journeys. For Nomo, coming to play in America is only one of the many challenges he's faced in his young life.

And it won't be his last.

Nomo looks in at the plate, takes the signal from Piazza, and goes into his windup. He thrusts his arms straight up and pushes out his chest. Then he pivots toward second base, his back momentarily facing Lofton at home plate. Finally, the "Tornado" whirls forward. And as the ball leaves Nomo's hand, dreams are coming true, and the future of baseball is looking a little brighter. With the speed of a fastball, things are changing. A Japanese baseball player is proving that he can compete with the best the world has to offer.

Six batters and two innings later, Nomo's job is done. The twenty-six-year-old rookie from Japan has just struck out three of the most feared hitters in the major league, including the speedy Lofton and the powerful Albert Belle. He has allowed only one hit, and, thanks to a double play, he has faced the minimum number of batters.

Nomo walks off the mound at the end of the second inning to the cheers of the Texas fans. They might be diehard supporters of the American League, but they know greatness when they see it. Nomo walks to the dugout and sits down. He thinks about

The Most Valuable Player Award for the 66th Major League All-Star Game went to Jeff Conine of the Florida Marlins. Conine hit the game-winning home run for the National League, who won the game 3 to 1. Appearances by Hideo Nomo, Carlos Perez, and Tyler Green marked the first time in All-Star history that three rookies played for the National League.

his dreams of pitching in the major leagues, of coming to America to play against the best. A subtle smile plays across his face as he realizes his dream has come true. And he wonders how he got here.

CHAPTER 2

Father and Son

In the beginning there were games of catch in the park. There was a father, Shizuo, who liked to tell baseball stories. And there was his very big son, Hideo.

Hideo Nomo was born on August 31, 1968, in Konohana-ku, a crowded downtown district of Osaka, Japan's second-largest city. A large baby by Japanese standards, Hideo weighed eight pounds and one-half ounce at birth. "We thought he might grow up to be a wrestler," said Hideo's father, referring to the very popular and very large sumo wrestlers of Japan. Hideo's mother, Kayoko, was also impressed with the baby's size, and both parents hoped that their first child would bring joy and honor to their home.

The name *Hideo* was given to the boy after much thought. In Japanese, two words can be pronounced the

21

same way yet have different meanings. The word *ki*, for example, can mean both *spirit* or *tree*, depending upon the character used to write the word. Likewise the name *Hideo*, though always pronounced the same, may be written with different characters that have different meanings. The characters Mr. Nomo chose for *Hideo* mean *superb* and *man*. Taken as a whole, this *Hideo* means *hero*.

When Hideo was three years old, the family—which now included a second son, Eiji— moved to Minato-ku, a district in Osaka not far from Konohana-ku.

Hideo was five years old when his father started taking him to the park in Minato-ku to play catch. This is where the Nomo baseball story really begins. On work days, young Hideo

Japan is made up of a chain of islands called an *archipelago*. The island of Honshu, the largest in the chain, is home to many major cities, including Osaka, Hideo Nomo's birthplace. Tokyo is also located on the island of Honshu. It is Japan's capital and its largest city. Tokyo is home to several pro baseball teams, including the Yomiuri Giants and the Yakult Swallows.

would wait for his father to return home from his job delivering the mail for the postal service. When his father arrived home, Hideo would drop whatever he was doing and greet his father with, "Dad, let's go play catch."

Shizuo Nomo has always thought of his son as a big kid with a big appetite. Looking back on Hideo's childhood, he described his son as a "very healthy boy who ate everything. He was such a big kid," he recalled, "that I thought playing catch in the park as often as possible would be a good thing for him."

Mr. Nomo was very concerned about his son's diet. He was a strong believer in vitamin A and made sure Hideo ate a lot of *unagi* (eel) and *sakana* (fish), foods rich in vitamin A. Hideo's mother would prepare the dishes, and Hideo seemed to thrive on them. Mr. Nomo thought that all the eel Hideo ate would make him grow up big and strong.

At bedtime, Shizuo would tell baseball stories to Hideo and his younger brother, Eiji. One of the players Mr. Nomo often talked about was Minoru Murayama. Mr. Nomo greatly admired Murayama, a local hero who played for the Osaka-based Hanshin Tigers in the 1960s and 1970s. Murayama was a popular player who had the honor of pitching before the Japanese emperor. One can easily imagine a young Hideo going to sleep with thoughts of Murayama's fastballs and fame swirling around in his head.

When Hideo was in the second grade, his father

bought him his first baseball glove. But the glove soon became a matter of concern for Mr. Nomo. "Hideo was putting all his energy into baseball," Mr. Nomo says of those years. "Even as a second grader, Hideo was very intense, a perfectionist."

Hideo once tore up a drawing of a baseball player he'd worked on because it was not realistic enough. Mr. Nomo began to worry. He felt that his child was a little too involved with baseball, that Hideo should have other interests. He sent him to a tutor who taught classical Japanese calligraphy, artistic handwriting that is done with a brush and ink. He also found Hideo a math tutor to help him with

Before World War II, Japanese Emperor Hirohito was believed to be a god. He was never seen in public—and certainly never at a baseball game. After the devastation of the war, however, the Emperor's role in Japanese society changed, and he became more accessible to the public. Emperor Hirohito attended many ball games and was often photographed in the stands.

his studies. But Hideo stayed with the classes only a short time, his focus always shifting back to baseball. Mr. Nomo fretted about his son's future. After all, only a handful of players could make a living from baseball, and it was too early to count Hideo among them.

In those early years, Mr. Nomo passed on much of his baseball knowledge to Hideo when the two played catch in the park. Aside from being a fan of the game, Mr. Nomo himself had played in a neighborhood league when he was younger. He taught Hideo to use his whole body when he pitched. This helped to increase ball speed. Hideo was a fast learner. According to Mr. Nomo, "By the time Hideo finished third grade, he was throwing like a sixth grader."

As a fifth grader, Hideo's talent was observed by a neighbor who suggested the budding pitcher sign up for Little League. Hideo tried out and soon became a pitcher for his first team, the Ikeshima Fire. (Because baseball was imported from the United States, most Japanese teams have English nicknames—such as the Giants, the Dragons, the Carp, and the Hawks.) Even in fifth grade he threw hard, harder than the other boys his age. But he was wild.

In sixth grade, Hideo was asked to write an essay on what he wanted to be when he grew up. Not surprisingly, he wrote, "I want to be a professional baseball player." Once again his father was concerned about his son. He wanted Hideo's wish to come true, but he didn't know if his son had the necessary talent. And he didn't want Hideo to be disappointed.

In seventh grade, the father-and-son ritual of playing catch in the park ended. "I could not tell him then," said Shizuo. "But he threw so hard that I was afraid to catch him! He threw with such force that he'd accidentally broken a bone in a teammate's hand."

In junior high school, Hideo trained long and hard. He especially liked to run. He felt that running would help develop his leg muscles, which, in turn, would help with his pitching velocity and control. He was a big kid who liked to eat—the running would help keep his weight down, too. Every morning he woke at 5:00 A.M. By 5:30 A.M. he would be aboard the train for school. The problem was that he trained so hard before school began, he sometimes fell asleep in class. In his early teens, Hideo had become totally dedicated to becoming a professional baseball player. Yet it was just that dedication, his focus only on training, that threatened to sideline his career.

Soon the time came for Hideo to enter high school. In America, high school students either go to the public school in their local area or to the private school that their parents have chosen for them. In contrast, Japanese students have to earn their assignment to a high school. They have to score high enough on a test to get into a good high school. The exams are tough, and students have to study very hard to get a good score. More than anything, Hideo wanted to attend Kindai Fuzoku, a high school with a great baseball team. Each year Kindai Fuzoku fielded a team good enough to participate in Japan's National High School Championship.

The tournament takes place in Osaka Prefecture twice yearly, in the spring and summer, and is held at the massive Koshien Stadium in Nishinomiya. Across the country, the tournament receives about as much attention as the NCAA Final Four basketball tournament does in the United States. The winners of the championship are honored nationally in the Japanese press. Japanese pro baseball teams scout the tournament heavily; a good performance there might lead to an invitation to a professional tryout.

Baseball is not the only popular sport played in Japan. Sumo wrestling—a sport that features surprisingly agile, 300-pound-and-over athletes—has always been a favorite among the Japanese. Soccer is also very popular. It is played on the professional level and by kids of all ages. And, in a nation of extremely hard workers, golf has found an avid following.

In Japan it is every high school player's dream to play in the celebrated tournament. Only the best teams—the ones that train year-round and field the most talented players—are invited to the tournament. And Kindai Fuzoku High often received an invitation.

In ninth grade, Hideo took the Kindai Fuzoku entrance exam and failed. Shocked and disappointed, he turned to his father for advice.

Shizuo Nomo pointed out the importance of education. If Hideo wanted to get anywhere, he would have to study more. Books would have to come before bats and balls. It was at this time Hideo began to study almost as hard as he trained.

Next, Hideo took the entrance exam for another school, Seijyo Kogyo. The school had never made it to the baseball tournament, but it did have something the teenage Nomo needed: an understanding coach named Akio Miyazaki. Hideo passed the exam and entered Seijyo Kogyo in 1983.

Akio Miyazaki was the school's mechanical engineering teacher. In the classroom he taught his students how things meshed and moved, how machines could work with minimum friction and maximum power. He was also the school's baseball coach, and there too, his concerns centered on movement, motion, and power. A team needed to mesh, and to win, there could be little friction.

The first time Hideo tried out for Miyazaki's team, he didn't make it. Hideo ran so hard in warmups, he was worn out by the time the tryout began. But he learned from this experience, and in the next tryout, he made the team.

Miyazaki coached Hideo for four years and remembers him as a shy and modest teenager. "He was considerate, always the first to congratulate his teammates—a quiet, but sweet kid," Coach Miyazaki said.

"Hideo trained harder than any of his teammates," said Coach Miyazaki, recalling how his star pitcher's abilities began to mature. "He was heavier than the other players, so he ran as much as seven miles every day." The coach said that all the running and the strength that came with his size made young Hideo a force to be reckoned with. Soon, Hideo was the "fastest pitcher in Osaka."

Miyazaki was a wise coach. He realized that the source of Hideo's pitch speed was his windup. Many other Japanese baseball coaches would have forced Hideo to pitch the "right" way even if it made his pitches slower. "It was an unusual windup," Coach Miyazaki said, referring to the way Hideo twists his body toward second base before whirling back toward home plate and delivering his pitch. "But I didn't want to change it. His delivery was not as exaggerated as it is today, but it was similar," said Miyasaki. This was the first sighting of Nomo's trademark Tornado windup.

Often Shizuo Nomo would come to the games to see his son pitch. As he watched from the grandstand, he was impressed with Hideo's increased control and the positive influence Coach Miyazaki was having on his son. Soon the coach and the father became friends.

Playing in a summer league in 1985, the future whirlwind finally touched down. Hideo pitched a perfect game—no runs, no hits, no walks, and no errors. Although he didn't pitch in the National High School Championship, the perfect game was Hideo's chance to be noticed. It was recorded in the newspapers, and professional scouts were made aware of Hideo. He was only sixteen. Hideo's quiet dedication had brought him a long way.

CHAPTER 3

HERO IN THE MAKING

Nomo's first name, Hideo, means hero. But if Nomo was to claim the title, "hero," he would have to earn it. There would be no miracles. There would be obstacles he would have to overcome. He needed to become an apprentice to baseball, absorbing the teachings of his coaches and studying the moves of teammates.

Nomo and his unusual windup were first discovered by a scout for Shin-nittetsu Sakai, one of Japan's Industrial League teams. The perfect game Nomo pitched in high school had brought him the attention he needed to take his first step on a long journey to pro baseball. After graduating in 1986, Nomo pursued his baseball dreams in Japan's Industrial League.

The Industrial League is kind of like A-level minor league ball in America, with one exception: The teams have no affiliation with any of Japan's twelve professional teams.

The Industrial League consists of teams sponsored by different corporations. The players all hold jobs with the companies and play baseball in addition to their work. The Osaka-based company Nomo played for, Shin-nittetsu Sakai, is part of a large steel-producing corporation. Nomo received a salary of about $1,200 per month. Half the day he worked in a factory, the other half on the field. In those days Nomo lived in a dorm with some of his teammates. He loved cars and used some of his salary to buy a Honda Civic. But that was about the only luxury his budget would allow.

Nomo was not a starting pitcher at first. He still was heavy, weighing more than 220 pounds. His coach, Yoshihiro Nakagawa, urged Nomo to bring his weight down to less than 200 pounds. He also suggested that Nomo begin developing more tools for his pitching arsenal. Nomo's fastball had plenty of speed, but it did not break up, down, right, or left. Through high school this straight fastball hadn't hurt Nomo. But even the best fastball can be hit by a good batter if it's thrown on a straight line.

In his first outing for Shin-nittetsu Sakai, Nomo was called in as a relief pitcher in the late innings of a close game. His first pitch was smacked for a home run—the winning home run. Nomo's confidence was at a low point. He'd suffered a major setback, and he'd have to learn from it.

Baseball stadiums in Japan look more like those in North America than you might think. Like the ballparks around the United States and Canada, the ballparks in Japan are fairly diverse; they range from modern to classical and large to small. The homes of the Yomiuri Giants and the Nippon Ham Fighters (who share Tokyo Dome) and the Daiei Hawks (who play in Fukuoka Dome) have quite modern appearances. As their stadium names communicate, they are space age-like domes enclosing ballparks. Other teams play in more old-fashioned, smaller ballparks. The Yokohama BayStars, for example, play in cozy Yokohama Stadium, which has a capacity of only 30,000. (The more modern parks hold between 48,000 and 50,000 fans.)

What is different about Japanese stadiums? Their home-run walls are not quite as far as the walls in parks in the U.S. and Canada. To hit a home run to center field in Green Stadium in Kobe, Japan, for example, a batter would have to hit the ball four hundred feet—that's a few feet less than he would have to hit a ball in the major league ballparks in North America.

Nomo's father hoped his son would continue to work hard and persevere, especially during tough times. "I always knew that Hideo would not make it on talent alone," he said. "But the years of hard work just might pay off."

In his three years playing in the Industrial League, Nomo learned how to pitch, and he practiced his craft with diligence and intensity. All the while, his coach helped him keep his weight down and his spirits up. And the problem arising from his straight fastball was also addressed. Nomo found a friend and teacher in teammate Nobuhire Shimizu, a fellow pitcher who taught the rookie how to throw a forkball.

As in American and Canadian ballparks, the ballparks in Japan sell a variety of snacks for the hungry baseball fan. You *may* see fans nibbling on peanuts, potato chips, or even hot dogs. But, chances are, fans in Japanese stadiums will more likely be chowing down on dried squid, *sushi* (sliced fish, often raw, on vinegared rice), or *udon* (thick noodles usually marinated in soy paste), soup, rice, or *yakitori* (grilled chicken on a skewer).

The forkball is a difficult pitch. It's nearly impossible to throw unless the pitcher's hand is large enough to hold the ball between his first and middle fingers. But it's a great pitch if one can throw it. The two-finger grip on the ball reduces the spin, causing the ball to dip. To the batter, the pitch looks like a fastball. But as it approaches the plate, it suddenly drops, hopefully fooling the hitter and making him swing at air. The forkball became Nomo's "out pitch," a pitch that could get him out of difficult situations. But it didn't come easy. Nomo practiced throwing forkballs constantly. And it still took him an entire year to master.

Larry Fuhrmann is an American sportswriter and broadcaster who has lived in Japan since 1982. He has watched Nomo evolve into an international sports star. "Nomo always was different," Fuhrmann said. "Coaches throughout his career never made him change his dynamic pitching motion. And it was in the Industrial League that his style developed further."

"Pitchers are nonconfrontational in Japan," Fuhrmann observes. "They all use the same motion. They nibble around the edges of the plate, work the count, and never go after hitters with power pitches. That's what makes Nomo different. Nomo is a power pitcher."

It was while playing in the Industrial League that Nomo first met Kikuko, his future wife. The coach of a rival team, for which Kikuko was employed as an assistant, introduced the two before one of their games. Shy and tongue-tied, Nomo somehow managed to bow and mumble his name to the young woman. Nomo was so taken by Kikuko's beauty and charm that he knew almost immediately he wanted to marry her. After the two said goodbye, Nomo hoped to have the opportunity of seeing her again soon.

Soon Nomo began to really shine in the Industrial League. Playing in the city tournament in 1988, Nomo started against a formidable ATT Tokyo club on July 30, going the distance and earning a 3 to 2 win. Four days later, he pitched an astonishing seventeen innings, beating the Fuji City team 2 to 1. After these performances, fans and pro scouts began asking, "Who is this guy?" Nomo's team failed to win the tournament, but Nomo's fastball and forkball were no longer a secret to Japan's baseball world.

His performances in the Industrial League earned Nomo a spot on the 1988 Japanese Olympic team. The kid from Osaka had definitely taken off. He was pitching against the world's best amateur players. The Japanese team received a silver medal in the 1988 Olympic Games in Seoul, South Korea.

After a final season in the Industrial League, Nomo set out on the next leg of a journey that would one day take him across the Pacific to Los Angeles. He was signed by a Japanese professional baseball team.

Hideo Nomo pitched for the Japanese national team in the 1988 Summer Olympics in Seoul, South Korea. His first appearance was in relief against the host team of South Korea. Japan won that game 3 to 1. In his second Olympic appearance, Nomo started against Taiwan and went 6⅔ innings for a 4 to 3 win. In his last outing in Seoul, Nomo again pitched in relief. The Japanese team lost that game 5 to 3 to the American team who went on to win the Olympic gold medal.

○　○　○

Hideo Nomo was the number-one pick of the Kintetsu Buffaloes in the 1989 amateur draft. American baseball fans might think that Kintetsu is a city and the Buffaloes are that city's team. Actually very few Japanese baseball teams are named for the cities where they play. Instead they are named for the companies that own them. Kintetsu is a railway company,

Baseball has a different flavor in Japan, and it's not just the hot dogs. Stadiums are smaller. The strike zone is higher. And on the pro level there are only twelve teams, compared to twenty-eight in America's major leagues.

The teams are divided into two leagues—the Central and the Pacific (Nomo's Buffaloes are in the Pacific League).

Basic Japanese coaching strategy includes, among other things, the importance of scoring the first run of the game. It is thought that the team that gives up the first run loses face, or credibility, a concept deeply rooted in Japanese philosophy.

Jim Nishi, sports editor for the Tokyo-based English-language newspaper the *Daily Yomiuri*, says, "In the United States, baseball is more of a power game than it is in Japan. In Japan pitchers have better control."

Like the American and National Leagues in the United States, Japan's Central and Pacific Leagues have slightly different playing rules. There is a commissioner's office, which, as in America, sets league schedules and organizes the draft. Unlike in America, however, each team in Japan is owned and controlled by a major corporation. The most popular team, the Yomiuri Giants, is owned by a newspaper and television conglomerate (in the United States it would be like naming the Atlanta Braves the "Turner Broadcasting Braves").

The Chiba Lotte Marines of the Pacific Coast League are owned by a gum and candy company. (Of course, for many years the Wrigley family—of Wrigley's chewing gum fame—owned the Chicago Cubs.) The Kintetsu Buffaloes are owned by the Kintetsu Railway Company. (The nearest railway stop to the Buffaloes' home field is serviced by the Kintetsu line.)

Although Japanese team owners are against sending homegrown players abroad to play for foreign teams, they are in favor of hiring players from other countries to play on *their* teams. Each Japanese professional team is allowed to carry three foreign players on its roster. Since 1950 more than four hundred foreigners have played, managed, or coached in Japan. Stars like Bill Madlock, Cecil Fielder, Bob Horner, Doug Decinces, Mell Hall, and Kevin Mitchell have all played in Japan.

Many Americans who played in Japan had trouble adjusting to the rigid training methods, the Japanese language, and the local cuisine. But all have been well paid for their troubles and efforts. And despite some Japanese coaches' beliefs that American players do not have the "correct team spirit," some American ball players have thrived in Japan. One American, Bobby Valentine, even managed in Japan. The manager's job—whether in Japan or America—is virtually the same. From the first days of spring training, he is charged with directing the team in practice and in games.

Spring training in Japan is really more like winter training. It begins on February 1, in the midst of the Japanese winter. Clubs in northern Japan provide handwarmers so the players can grip their bats and balls properly. Japanese teams practice year-round, with only a week off after Japan's World Series, which is played in late October.

Hideo Nomo's first "spring" training was in 1990. Fortunately for Nomo his preseason training was held on Saipan, a tropical island in the western Pacific that is technically part of the United States. There, among the coconut palms and rice fields, Nomo began his first stint in professional baseball.

Japanese coaches are a strict bunch, conducting spring training sessions much like army drill sergeants at boot camp. Many managers believe that hard work is the key to winning, and that individual talent is not as important as team unity and effort. This approach to the game differs from the approach taken in American baseball. But that doesn't mean it is any better or worse. It is simply different.

Training for Japanese pitchers is particularly rough. Players are put through a set of grueling windsprints and calisthenics followed by painful stretching exercises. Meals are often eaten on the field during breaks. Pitchers are expected to throw more than 400 pitches per day. (A typical nine-inning American game averages 120 pitches.) Complaints about sore arms are not accepted. Relief pitchers are used more sparingly in Japan. Needless to say, in Japanese baseball, pitcher burnout is a serious problem.

Japanese pitchers are trained to throw more sidearm than their American counterparts, and emphasis is placed on the curveball, not the fastball. Hideo Nomo throws closer to over the top and prefers fastballs. "As

Japanese players go, Nomo was always atypical," sports-writer Fuhrmann said.

After the first few weeks in spring training, Nomo worked his way into the Buffaloes' starting rotation.

"There has always been a fire burning inside of him, to prove he was the best in his profession," Fuhrmann said.

The day to prove himself would soon come.

○   ○   ○

Surrounded by classical-looking white columns, Fujidera Stadium, located between Osaka and Nara, is one of the smaller stadiums in Japan. Fujidera seats only 32,000 fans and features particularly short right- and left-field lines (only 298 feet for a home run). Inside the stadium, the spectator is treated to the usual base-ball landscape—dirt infields and artificial turf. This is the field where Nomo made his first Pacific League start.

In most Japanese stadiums the bullpens are located under the stands or surrounded by high brick walls. Not so at Fujidera. The bullpens are open, and the play-ers are easily viewed by the fans. That day the specta-tors in Fujidera Stadium watched with curiosity as the rookie pitcher warmed up.

Before Nomo's first start, there were the usual activi-ties that usher in a Japanese baseball game: Cheerleaders leading the crowd in songs; fans blowing horns and clapping rhythmically; and the stadium organist playing the home team's song. No one is looking at a program or a scorecard, though—there aren't any. Instead, spectators purchase guides to match players' names with their jerseys. And the stadium announcers, in contrast to those in the United States, are often women.

That day in Fujidera, Hideo Nomo took the mound for his first start. It was April 10, 1990. The crowd clapped and cheered in anticipation. The new season was only a couple of weeks old, and the fans were enthusiastic about their team's chances. Not since 1980 had the Buffaloes won the Pacific League title. And many wondered if this would be their year. There were rumors that a new wind would bring change to their fortunes. There had been stories in the press about a potential new star for their team.

The Japanese press covers baseball extensively. Statistics. Box scores. Rumors. Scandals. And in 1990, the arrival of an Olympic silver medalist had not been overlooked. The crowd had come to see if Nomo could deliver.

It was Nomo's first pro start, but it was not his day. Although he pitched six strong innings, Nomo and the Buffaloes lost to the Seibu Lions 5 to 2. Over the next two weeks and two starts, Nomo gained in experience and confidence, but he was still without his first win. Then, on April 29, Nomo made his fourth start of the year. It

The twelve Japanese professional baseball teams are divided into two divisions.

CENTRAL LEAGUE	**PACIFIC LEAGUE**
Yomiuri Giants (Tokyo)	Seibu Lions (Tokorozawa)
Chunichi Dragons (Nagoya)	Orix BlueWaves (Kobe)
Hiroshima Toyo Carp (Hiroshima)	Kintetsu Buffaloes (Osaka)
Yakult Swallows (Tokyo)	Fukuoka Daiei Hawks (Fukuoka)
Hanshin Tigers (Nishinomiya)	Chiba Lotte Marines (Chiba)
Yokohama BayStars (Yokohama)	Nippon Ham Fighters (Tokyo)

was against the Orix Braves at Nishinomiya Stadium, and it was Nomo's first win as a pro.

That day, to the delight of the fans, his parents, and all those who had coached and trained him, Nomo methodically struck out seventeen batters, tieing a longstanding Japanese record. He pitched a complete game, and the Buffaloes won 2 to 0. Nomo won the game and the fans' hearts.

In his rookie season in the pros, Hideo Nomo became what his father always hoped he would be, a baseball hero.

CHAPTER 4

TORNADO SEASONS

Nomo's eye-catching fourth game with the Kintetsu Buffaloes was only the first of his many accomplishments that year. In his first season with the Buffaloes, Nomo struck out an astonishing 287 batters in 235 innings—more than one strikeout per inning! Nomo finished his season with a record of eighteen wins and eight losses and a low earned run average (ERA) of 2.91.

His first year in the Pacific League, Nomo also had a chance to pitch against American major leaguers. For years a team of major league All Stars has traveled to Japan to play a series of exhibition games against Japanese pro teams. Pitching in three relief appearances, Nomo's record was 1-1.

As the season progressed, fan interest in Nomo's unique windup increased. The Buffaloes were eager to popularize their rising star. Noting the curiosity generated by his unusual windup, Buffaloes management organized a write-in contest to give Nomo's twisting windup a name. Winner? "Tornado," of course.

In his rookie Pacific League Season, Nomo was named 1990 Most Valuable Player and Rookie of the Year. He also won the prestigious *Sewamura* Award—equivalent to the major leagues' Cy Young Award—which is given each year to the best pitcher.

During his first year in the pros, his commitment to Kikuko deepened. Shortly thereafter, the couple held a press conference where they officially announced their engagement.

The Buffaloes' manager, Ogi Kantoku, had been the one who'd pursued Nomo for the team. For Nomo, playing for Ogi was like a dream. Coach Ogi agreed not to alter his star pitcher's now-trademark style, and he also introduced Nomo to the modern training methods of one of the team's pitching coaches, Ryuji Tachibana.

Tachibana was a disciple of the Osaka Dynamic Sports Medical Laboratory, a local training and research facility. While there, he studied all aspects of modern physical conditioning so vital to athletes, including diet and muscle development. Soon, Nomo became a follower of these methods as well. Some days coach and player would train at the ballpark, others they would go to the "Lab" to work out. A relationship based on trust and mutual respect developed between the two men.

Tachibana, according to Larry Fuhrmann, was also a trainer who "admired American methods of training." Tachibana actually traveled to the United States one year to interview Nolan Ryan and ask the veteran power pitcher about his training methods. During his trip, the coach fulfilled another mission. He asked Ryan for a jersey to take back to his star pupil. When he returned to Japan, Tachibana gave Nomo a jersey bearing the name of *his* hero.

That year, Nomo found a fiancée, a team, a coach, and a nickname. It was his year. Yet he was still denied one thing—the Buffaloes failed to take the Pacific League pennant.

Athletes are not the only talented Japanese individuals who have moved west in an attempt to further their professional careers. Seiji Ozawa, a prominent symphony conductor, born in Japan in 1935, moved west to become a conductor of both the Toronto Symphony in Canada and the San Francisco Symphony Orchestra in California, as well as the musical director of the Boston Symphony Orchestra.

The disappointment faded quickly. And before the next season began, Nomo had accomplished something very special. In 1991, he and Kikuko were married.

His second year with the Buffaloes, Nomo won seventeen games and lost eleven, posting an ERA of 3.05. But that was just part of the story. Nomo's seventeen wins and 287 strikeouts were league-leading numbers. And he was selected to Japan's 1991 All-Star team. But still no pennant for the Buffaloes.

The Tornado's third year in the pros (1992) was just as impressive as his first two. He won eighteen games, losing eight, with an ERA of 2.66. He pitched seventeen complete games and threw a career-high five shutouts. Nomo struck out 228 batters in 216 innings. That year Nomo had another opportunity to pitch against the traveling Major League All-Star team, which visited Japan in October and November. He lost one game and had two no-decisions, striking out eleven in eight innings. Another great year. But no playoffs.

The 1992 season saw yet another milestone for the Nomo family. That year Kikuko gave birth to a baby boy, Takahiro—an event more important to the quiet couple than records or playoffs.

Each year Nomo's interest in American baseball grew. When he pitched in the traveling All-Star series, the American and Japanese players exchanged their jerseys when the series ended. One year Nomo traded his with Dave Stewart, a power pitcher formerly with the

Oakland A's. Another year, Roger Clemens, the Boston Red Sox fireballer, traded jerseys with Nomo. "At the time," says Fuhrmann, "I wonder if the Americans thought they were getting the short end of the trade."

Fuhrmann, who followed Nomo's career closely during his years with Kintetsu, has had the opportunity to meet Nomo up close and personal. He describes the Japanese pitching star as a "simple guy" who doesn't like controversy. "He has his own opinions about things, but he prefers to keep them to himself." Fuhrmann, who speaks fluent Japanese, remembers dining with the then-Buffaloes' star at an American-style sports bar. Nomo didn't say much. "He likes to have fun. But he's more on the quiet side," Fuhrmann says.

Saying little has become a trademark of Nomo's career. A reluctant celebrity, he prefers speaking to the press solely about the task at hand—winning ball games. He has always been of the opinion that "the press writes about too many private things." This view creates friction between Nomo and baseball journalists. But Nomo insists he has nothing against the press. He just wants to play ball and enjoy a private life with his family and friends.

Nomo's fourth season with the Kintetsu Buffaloes was yet another banner year. He led the Pacific League in wins, 17, and strikeouts, 276. By early 1994, Nomo reached the 1,000 career strikeout mark. He achieved that milestone faster than any pitcher in Japanese baseball

Keishi Suzuki led Japan's Pacific League in strikeouts for six straight years (1967–1972) when he pitched for the Kintetsu Buffaloes. He had a fine fastball and was able to spot it exactly where he wanted. In his lifetime, he earned 317 wins and 238 losses with 3,061 strikeouts. In 1994, while Nomo was with the team, Suzuki was named manager of the Buffaloes. He coached the team for two seasons and was released after the Buffaloes, now without Nomo, finished the 1995 season in last place.

history. It was another year of personal triumph for Nomo, but again, no postseason play.

Toward the end of the 1993 season, the usually private Nomo found himself included in a public debate. In 1993, the Buffaloes hired a new manager, former pitching star Keishi Suzuki. In the 1960s and 1970s, Suzuki, like Nomo, was a dominating pitcher. In fact, it was Suzuki's record of forty-three double-digit strikeout games, accumulated over twenty years, that Nomo had broken in only three years. And now Nomo was his student, and Suzuki would train the team—and pitching staff—his way.

Trained in the old school of Japanese baseball, Suzuki was a tough-minded manager. Almost immediately there was trouble between the new coach and his star. One of Suzuki's first moves was to fire Tachibana, Nomo's friend, trainer, and pitching coach—a man whom Nomo credited with much of his success. Coach Suzuki didn't appreciate Tachibana's nontraditional training methods.

The tension between coach and pitcher continued into the 1994 season. Suzuki was a man who insisted on doing things his way. "Little things became big issues," said Fuhrmann. "Nomo preferred to do his training in running shoes; Suzuki insisted he run in spikes. . . . Nomo and Suzuki did not get along."

Then things got worse. Nomo came down with a sore right arm and shoulder. Suzuki, old schooler that he was, would have none of this. Traditionally, Japanese baseball coaches deal with an injured player by urging him to play through the injury. Midway through the season, however, Nomo's arm was shot. He could pitch no more. Rumors spread that Nomo would soon be traded. Suddenly the baseball career Nomo had taken so long to cultivate was dissolving right before his eyes.

In his fifth and final year with the Kintetsu Buffaloes, Nomo started seventeen games, winning eight and losing seven, with an ERA of 3.63. In his five years with the Buffaloes he had averaged more than one strikeout per inning, a staggering figure for a starting pitcher. He was a famous baseball player, yet his future was in serious doubt.

But Nomo had reached the point of no return with Japanese baseball. It was evident that Nomo and Suzuki could not work on the same team. Even if Nomo's arm recovered in time to play the 1995 season, Suzuki had suggested to the press that he'd bench Nomo.

The Tornado sought the advice of a baseball agent who was well connected to Japanese baseball. The agent's name was Donald Nomura. Nomura had represented another Japanese player, Mac Suzuki, and had gotten him a contract with the Seattle Mariners, where he was working his way up through the club's minor league system. Nomo had to decide: Was he ready to play in America? He had always dreamed of testing his skills overseas against the major leaguers. He'd admired them so much since he was a kid. And he had proved he could get them out. But a major league contract never seemed possible—until now.

None of Nomo's close friends or family members thought he should play baseball in America. His wife wasn't crazy about the idea, nor was his father. At the time of his season-ending injury, Nomo was earning more than $1.5 million per season. His father and friends thought that if his dream was to play in America, he should find another dream. And it wasn't only about the money he was making.

Why?

Like many other countries, Japan is a homogeneous nation, which means that most Japanese share the same racial, ethnic, and religious background. Though they accept and embrace many things from the United States and other Western countries, such as clothing, music, and baseball, many Japanese people strongly maintain their own ways and traditions. This can be explained in part by Japan's history. Japan is an isolated island nation, and as recently as 140 years ago, its people rarely had any contact with the outside world. It's only natural that the people of such a nation should feel a strong bond with one another.

Nomo's family and advisors thought it odd for him to leave Japan to pitch in a place that had such different customs, language, and diet. How could he live in such a place? Other Japanese, especially business people, had returned from extended stays in the United States complaining of the lack of even the basic necessities. They had missed their home; they had missed the Japanese way of life. Even if Nomo succeeded and made the roster of a U.S. ball club, wouldn't he, too, soon miss his home? Imagine spending a year away from your home. Everyone looks different. The seasons and climate are different. The holidays you look forward to are not celebrated. No one speaks your language. You cannot even ask for directions or order a meal without an interpreter. Your favorite foods are not available. And your only contact with loved ones is by phone. Would you be lonely? Only a person with strong beliefs and confidence would make such a journey—or even think about it.

The American All-Stars had traveled far to play their Japanese counterparts. Was it now time for Nomo to meet them on their own turf? Was it time to switch from collecting major league jerseys to earning one of his own?

CHAPTER 5

CROSSING THE PACIFIC

One winter day in 1995, Hideo Nomo went to his parents' home in Osaka to tell them he was going to America. It was a decision that had taken a great deal of thought. Nomo's father remembers his son coming over that day and announcing his plans. "I'm going to the United States to play ball," Nomo announced.

"At the time I couldn't understand why he was doing this," Mr. Nomo explains. "He had a very comfortable life here. He was a big star."

The Kintetsu Buffaloes were paying Nomo more money per year than his father had made in a lifetime, and all for throwing a baseball. Mr. Nomo thought it was unthinkable to throw away such good fortune.

Mr. Nomo wanted to say no, but he couldn't tell his son not to do this thing. Besides, he saw the fire in

Nomo's eyes, the sheer joy that the mere thought of going to America brought to his son. He hadn't seen Nomo this alive in a long time. Mr. Nomo knew that if his son didn't chase this dream, it would eat at him for a long time. Reluctantly, he gave his blessing.

Hideo Nomo didn't just wake up one morning and decide to pitch in America. The decision took a lot of thought. He studied the problem. He talked with his wife. He planned. And his planning and study told him his best chance was to work with Don Nomura, the sports agent with contacts in American and Japanese baseball circles.

Nomura's background made him well suited to Nomo's quest. The son of an American father and a Japanese mother, Nomura was familiar with both cultures.

Nomura's mother divorced her first husband and later married former baseball star Katsuya Nomura, who adopted Don and raised him as his son. Like his father, Don Nomura also played professional baseball in Japan, with a minor league club, the Yakult Swallows. He grew dissatisfied with the strict approach of many Japanese coaches. It seemed natural that years later he would work to change Japanese baseball.

Hideo Nomo and Don Nomura found each other during Nomo's 1994 season of discontent. Nomura had already made a name for himself by becoming an agent in a land where agents were a rarity. He had already helped another ballplayer, Mac Suzuki, sign a contract with an American team. Building on that experience, Nomura met Nomo to discuss various ways that Nomo might leave Japanese baseball.

None was obvious. There were five years remaining on his current contract with the Buffaloes. The contract specifically prohibited Nomo from being traded to an American team. Nomo could quit the Buffaloes, but he was not allowed to play for another team until the five years were up.

Or so he thought.

Contracts are legal agreements made between people. They are worded very carefully,

One of Japan's greatest baseball heroes is Katsuya Nomura. Compact and powerful, this catcher was one of the first power hitters in Japanese baseball. Having met and studied a variety of American players during his career of more that 2,500 games, Nomura integrated a number of American techniques into his own game. In 1995, Nomura, now retired as a player, coached the Yakult Swallows to victory in the Japan World Series.

Nomo is not the first Japanese to move to the United States and play major league baseball. On September 1, 1964, Masanori Murakami, a left-handed pitcher for the San Francisco Giants, made his American major league debut. He pitched against the New York Mets at Shea Stadium. At this time, many thought that Murakami's excellent performance would spur a massive migration of Japanese players to the United States. Such a major migration, however, failed to occur. The second Japanese major leaguer, Hideo Nomo, didn't come until thirty years later.

Teammates and fans of Murakami remember him as an intense competitor with a warm heart and a winning record. He went one and zero his first season with the Giants and four and one with a 3.50 ERA his second season. In 1966, Murakami returned to Japan to finish out his baseball career. He played for seventeen more seasons back in his homeland.

but if a good lawyer searches hard enough, he or she may find some gap in the contract. Nomura knew there had to be a way to break Nomo's contract.

He called on the services of Arn Tellum, a West Coast sports agent and legal expert. He asked Tellum to examine Nomo's agreement with the Buffaloes, and Tellum was able to find a loophole (a way of getting around the rules laid down in the contract).

The contract said that Nomo couldn't *quit* and then join another team, but it didn't say anything about his *retiring* from the team. Tellum discovered that Nomo could retire from the Buffaloes, freeing himself from all obligations, and try to sign on with an American team.

To the shock of Japanese baseball fans, Hideo Nomo announced his retirement from baseball at the end of the 1994 season. He then announced that he was a free agent, able to negotiate a contract with *any* team. Coach Suzuki and the Buffaloes had underestimated Nomo. Nomo was earning between $1.5 and $2 million his last year with the Buffaloes, and still he walked away. Now he was free to play wherever he wanted. Embarrassed by the loss of his star pitcher, Buffaloes' General Manager Yasuo Maeda soon resigned.

Overnight, Nomo was the talk of Japanese baseball. His face was plastered on every front page of Japan's sports newspapers. Nomo was a baseball star, and he was often the target of stories good and bad in the Japanese papers, but now he was the sports story of the year.

There was fear in the Japanese commissioner's office as well—and it was justified. "The top twenty pitchers in Japan are all major league caliber or above," commented Bobby Valentine, the former Texas Ranger manager, who was managing Japan's Chiba Lotte Marines during the Nomo controversy. And indeed many executives of Japan's pro baseball teams were extremely anxious about the whole affair. Soon even the fans began to regard Nomo as a kind of traitor. And Nomura would never win a popularity contest with the Buffaloes management either. What if those top twenty pitchers *did* leave Japan for greener pastures? Where would Japanese baseball be then? Like it or not, the commissioner knew that the Nomo case had changed the rules of the game, and now he feared Japan's finest also might be heading west.

When asked for his thoughts on Nomo, Masaki Nagino, head of the Central League's planning department, replied, "As a professional baseball organization, we lost a kind of treasure."

Meanwhile, in America professional baseball eyes had been watching the Nomo affair with great interest. Many American teams needed pitchers; one of them was the Los Angeles Dodgers. And Dodgers' President Peter O'Malley was the kind of guy who liked to break new ground. He wanted Nomo.

It seemed fated that Hideo Nomo would sign with the Dodgers. Peter O'Malley has had an interest in foreign baseball since the 1950s, when Peter's father, Walter O'Malley, was the then-Brooklyn Dodgers' president. "My family and I visited our top farm team in Montreal, Canada," says O'Malley. "We also traveled to Havana, Cuba, and the Dominican Republic for spring training."

Following the 1956 World Series, O'Malley accompanied his father and the Brooklyn Dodgers on a thirty-day goodwill visit to Japan. There, the Dodgers played a series of exhibition games against Japanese professionals. On the trip, the Dodgers won fourteen, lost four, and tied once. "It was an extraordinary introduction for me to baseball in that country," O'Malley says. Over the years the Dodgers have sent scouts and coaches to many countries. But historically there seems to have been special interest in Japan. The Yomiuri (Tokyo) Giants have visited the United States five times, compiling a record of five wins, seven losses, and two ties against Dodger minor league teams, and the Chunichi (Nagoya) Dragons have visited once.

Peter O'Malley's interest in baseball has been truly global. In 1987 he founded Campo Las Palmas, a Dodger training facility located in the Dominican Republic, to develop Dominican ballplayers. Dodger Dominican alumni include star pitcher Ramon Martinez and 1994 Rookie of the Year Raul Mondesi. The most famous Dodger of recent years has also been a foreign find—Fernando Valenzuela, from Navojoa in the state of Sonora, Mexico. Valenzuela's success in 1981 created the fan phenomenon known as "Fernandomania."

For O'Malley, bringing players together from foreign lands to play for the Dodgers has been a goal and a dream. By early 1995, when Hideo Nomo announced his retirement from Japanese baseball, more than 40 percent of the Dodgers' minor league system was made up of players from foreign countries. To anyone who knew Peter O'Malley, his quick response to Nomo was not a surprise.

O O O

Hideo Nomo and his agent Don Nomura boarded a westbound jet on a mission to the United States. Both men knew that Nomo's skills were of value in Japan. Now they would see about the big leagues. Don Nomura, who speaks both English and Japanese and is a tough negotiator in either language, was the key to the plan's success.

If Nomo found work on an American team, his wife and son would follow him later in the season. Nomo had only been to the States once before, on a stopover in Florida. He knew no English; he had no relatives to call upon arrival. He had packed only his clothes, his glove, and his desire. In America, he and Nomura had to find him a home. A team. A place to unpack his glove and apply his desire.

Peter O'Malley called Nomura's office the first day Nomo's retirement cleared with Japanese baseball. He

Hideo Nomo will have no trouble finding Japanese food or Japanese culture while he is living in Los Angeles. Southern California is filled with the cultural marks of this East Asian nation. Japanese started immigrating to Southern California in the late 1800s. By 1907, Los Angeles had a distinct Japanese business district appropriately named "Little Tokyo."

Today, Nomo could watch classical Kabuki theater, sing along with a karaoke show, or take in some traditional Japanese music at the Japan America Theater, part of the Japanese Community and Cultural Center in downtown Los Angeles. Or, if Nomo wanted to talk sports, he could visit the Japan-U.S. Sports Foundation, an organization that promotes American and Japanese friendship and goodwill through sports—an appropriate place for this American-based Japanese baseball player to hang out. This foundation sponsors tournaments and clinics that introduce American sports to Japan and Japanese sports to the United States.

invited Nomura and his client to come to Los Angeles and talk about Nomo pitching for the Dodgers. The timing wasn't good.

Los Angeles was not Nomo's and Nomura's first stop on their trip to the United States. Their first meeting was with the Seattle Mariners of the American League, a team with whom Don Nomura had already done business. Nomo and the Mariners seemed to be a perfect match. One of the Mariners' owners was president of Nintendo America. Nintendo, the giant video game manufacturer, is a Japanese company. The president of Nintendo America is Japanese.

But the Mariners had problems. American baseball was on strike, and the Mariners had trouble drawing fans before the strike. Besides, the Mariners owners were threatening to leave Seattle if they didn't get a better stadium. Money was tight, and they didn't have any to risk on Nomo. No deal was struck.

Nomo's next stop was down the West Coast to San Francisco, home of the Giants and a large Japanese-American and Japanese population. The Giants thought Nomo would give their pitching staff a big boost. They even called upon a former Giants' pitcher, Masanori Murakami, the very first Japanese to play in the major leagues, to help persuade Nomo to join the team. But a deal could not be struck.

Now it was on to Los Angeles. The Dodgers' coaching staff had not seen Nomo pitch. They only knew him by reputation and a short video of Nomo's pitching highlights. "None of our scouts had seen him," said O'Malley. "But all the reports on him were good. We were told that he had a nasty forkball."

They also knew that Nomo sat out most of the 1994 season with a sore shoulder, an injury that prevented most teams from risking money on him. O'Malley decided to take a gamble. He offered Nomo $1 million to sign. Don Nomura told O'Malley they could get more elsewhere, and prepared to move on to an appointment with the New York Yankees. O'Malley didn't want to lose Nomo. He raised the Dodgers' bid to $2 million. On February 13, 1995, all parties were invited to Peter O'Malley's office in the upper deck of Dodger Stadium. The one-year deal included a $2 million signing bonus and a major league minimum starting salary of $109,000.

Nomo pulled a Dodger jersey bearing number sixteen over his shirt. The press took photos. It was a new beginning. Nomo had found a new baseball home in Los Angeles, a city with a large Japanese American population, a new Japanese American National Museum, and an area downtown known as Little Tokyo. The city of Los Angeles was a key factor in the deal. But when asked by reporters why he chose L.A., Nomo replied, "No other team had Peter O'Malley."

"We admire Mr. Nomo's decision to play baseball in the United States," says O'Malley. "He has been a

superstar in Japan and now has a dream to be success-
ful in the major leagues. We believe that he will make a
significant impact as a member of the Dodger team."

Nomo had landed. The deal was signed. Yet the
dream would have to wait.

Major league baseball was still on strike.

CHAPTER 6

ROOKIE IN AMERICA

The next stop on Nomo's journey through American baseball was Dodgertown. It was a stop well suited to a player from abroad. Located in Vero Beach, Florida, Dodgertown is a virtual global village of baseball.

Each spring, players from around the world—the Dominican Republic, Venezuela, Mexico, Korea, and elsewhere—are invited to Dodgertown to try to beat the odds and make the Dodger team. This spring Peter O'Malley's "United Nations of Baseball" increased its membership by one with the addition of Hideo Nomo.

But Nomo could not have chosen a worse time to come to America. A baseball players' strike was still on. The strike had begun August 12, 1994, and had wiped out the second half of the 1994 season. There were no pennant races in 1994. No playoffs. No World Series.

Curt Flood, an All-Star outfielder for the St. Louis Cardinals, was one of the first major leaguers to seriously challenge the terms of his baseball contract. As all baseball contracts at that time (before 1975), Flood's contract prohibited him from changing teams without the express consent of the owner of his current team. Represented by famous sports attorney Marvin Miller, Flood argued that once he had played with a team for a certain amount of time, he should earn free agency, that is, he should be able to sign with the team that offered him the most appealing deal.

The players and the owners couldn't agree on a number of contract-related issues. Because of their dispute with the owners, the players had refused to report to training camp. But the owners had the upper hand in the dispute. They managed the ballparks and on March 30, 1995, they voted twenty-six to two to lock out the players and begin spring training with replacement players.

It was an unusual spring training. When Nomo arrived in camp in the beginning of March, he was surrounded by replacement players, guys who normally would have little chance of making a pro team. They were carpenters, bus drivers, bartenders, and a lot of minor league players who had chosen to quit or temporarily leave their jobs to pursue a once-in-a-lifetime opportunity to play major league baseball.

But the arrival of replacement players in spring season created a special problem for Nomo. The United States Labor Department had issued a ruling prohibiting foreign players from serving as replacement players. As long as teams fielded replacement players, they could not sign Nomo. Until the strike ended, Nomo could only hope to be signed to a minor league team. Like everyone else who followed baseball, Nomo was unsure about how the season would progress.

While awaiting an answer, Nomo trained hard for both possibilities. There are seven practice fields on Dodgertown's landscaped grounds. The facility also includes a weight-training room, a swimming pool, tennis courts, and a golf course. Connecting this village is a network of roads named after Dodger greats from the past. While strolling down Duke Snyder Avenue, a player can daydream about driving a fastball over the center-field wall. And while jogging down Jackie Robinson Avenue, a player can dream about sliding into second base under the tag just as the loud screams of "ssssaaaaaffffe" erupt from the umpire.

As Nomo waited to find out when and if he would become a part of the major league Dodger tradition, dozens of reporters from the Japanese press corps also waited. It immediately became evident to Nomo that the Japanese baseball writers would shadow his every move in America. Since Nomo had announced back in Japan that he intended to play baseball in America, the press had been knocking him, publishing one nasty story after another. But from spring training on, their attitude toward Nomo began to change, and now the Japanese press was behind their native son.

American baseball writers were also beginning to awaken to this story. And to help Nomo in his dealings with day-to-day language challenges, the Dodgers hired Michael Okumura as his interpreter.

At twenty-eight, Okumura had the experience for the job. Born in Tokyo in 1967, Okumura moved to the Los Angeles area in 1986. He had studied English in Japan and continued his studies at Santa Monica City College in Southern California. His first job as an interpreter was in 1990, with the Salinas Spurs, a minor league baseball team partly owned by Nomo's agent, Don Nomura. At the time, Okumura interpreted for Mac Suzuki, another of Nomura's clients.

How close was Okumura to Nomo at Dodgertown? "In spring training we shared a room," Okumura says. "I was with him twenty-four hours a day."

Nomo came to camp needing to recover arm strength and pitching form from the previous season's injury. In his first few days in spring training, he was introduced to Pat Screnar, the Dodgers' physical therapist. Nomo's shoulder needed work, and he also needed to lose some weight.

"Nomo knew very little English," says Okumura. "My most important job was taking Nomo to Pat Screnar for arm stretching and arm strengthening. It was extremely important to make sure that there were no miscommunications between the two."

Soon Nomo's arm grew stronger, and according to Okumura, he lost about five pounds. "He was working hard and getting in great shape," comments Okumura. At mealtimes, Nomo and Okumura would eat together. "He didn't want the Dodgers

As of February 1995, 106 out of 246 players in the Dodger organization were from other countries—that's 43 percent of the organization's players. Countries represented included (number in parentheses is the number of players from the country): the Dominican Republic (66), Venezuela (11), Ecuador (1), Mexico (8), Australia (3), Brazil (1), Canada (1), Cuba (1), Germany (1), Guatemala (1), Japan (1), Korea (1), and the Netherlands (1).

to prepare Japanese meals for him," says Okumura. "He wanted to eat the same food as the other players."

Okumura also would interpret between Nomo and Dodger pitching coach Dave Wallace when Nomo practiced in the bullpen. Wallace's guidance would prove critical to Nomo's success in the majors. "We evaluated his pitching at the beginning of the season," Wallace said, "and asked him to throw a little lower. The strike zone is lower here than in Japan."

To learn how to throw the "low strike," Nomo worked out in the camp's string area, a batter's box outfitted with string marking the zones of balls and strikes.

After practices Nomo ran, doing more than twenty minutes of sprints between the foul line and center field. Comments Wallace, "Nomo is absolutely motivated. He is one player you don't have to watch to make sure he stays with the training program."

Coach Wallace knew some basic expressions in Japanese, at least enough to make Okumura's job a little easier. "Essential phrases," according to Wallace. "Keep the ball down. Are you in pain? Throw inside. Throw outside."

In evaluating Nomo, Coach Wallace had this to say: "Nomo has the total package. He has a good fastball and a good forkball. He is intelligent. He studies the hitters and is very competitive."

Nomo's batting skills, however, were not so refined. Probably for the first time in many seasons, Nomo took batting practice in Dodgertown. As in the American League, Japan's Pacific League observes the designated hitter rule, which means pitchers don't bat. However, there is no designated hitter in the National League. For the first time in his pro career, Nomo would have to stand in the batter's box and swing away at another hurler's ninety-mile-per-hour fastballs and head-spinning curves. It's not as easy as it looks.

Although Nomo was growing more confident as spring training progressed, he was still nervous about his baseball future. No one knew if there would even be a major league season. The Japanese press corps in Florida was growing—and they were growing more demanding. About every four days Nomo held a press conference to appease them. But the press wanted more access. Even with Okumura's help, the press was becoming a distraction for Nomo. "During those first weeks, all Nomo wanted to do was focus on baseball," Okumura says. The press wouldn't let him.

Finally on April 2, 1995, the strike was over. The replacement players were sent home. And although the owners and players weren't able to agree to new terms, they did agree *not* to lose another season to labor squabbles. They decided to put off their talks long enough to jump-start major league baseball.

Baseball was back. The season that was supposed to have started April 1 was postponed for two weeks, two weeks for the real players to practice for the season.

everal American Dodgers of various American racial and ethnic backgrounds have played crucial roles in breaking down racial barriers or biases within professional baseball. Jackie Robinson was the first African American ever to play in the major leagues. Dodger pitcher Sandy Koufax not only emerged as one of the greatest pitchers in the history of baseball, he also was one of the few Jewish players to have played in the major leagues. And, more recently, Mexican pitcher Fernando Valenzuela became one of the Dodgers' biggest stars when he joined the team in the 1980s.

Once spring training games got under way, Nomo, the rookie wearing number sixteen, saw his first action in America. In two games he pitched eleven innings. He struck out an awesome eleven batters, but gave up eleven walks as well. The Tornado just couldn't get used to the National League strike zone.

Nomo was assigned to Albuquerque, the Dodgers' AAA minor league club, for more practice. But just before the season began, he was called to pitch for the Bakersfield Blades, another club in the Dodgers' farm system. The game was played in Rancho Cucamonga, near Los Angeles, home to the Cucamonga Quakes. Okumura remembers the outing as a "very good one for Nomo." In five innings he struck out six and walked only one.

Nomo had impressed Coach Wallace and Manager Lasorda enough to be named to the Dodgers' starting rotation, along with Ramon Martinez, Tom Candiotti, and Ismael Valdes.

The 1995 season began on April 25. A week later, the Dodgers were off to a record of three wins and three losses, and Nomo was about to make his first major league start.

In his first game, on May 2, Nomo would face powerhouse Barry Bonds and the San Francisco Giants. It was ironic that his first start would be in San Francisco—the city where Masanori Murakami, the only other Japanese player to play in the major leagues, pitched a generation earlier.

Candlestick Park, located near Hunters Point in San Francisco, is on the edge of the Pacific Ocean—the shore opposite Nomo's home in Japan. During some games, the ocean fog rolls into the park and obscures play. Yet, fog would not dampen the interest that accompanied Nomo's first start in America. But that interest was somewhat delayed, however.

In fact, Nomo's first game somehow remained a secret to the Giants. "The Dodgers didn't let us know that he was going to pitch," recalls Jim Moorehead, media relations director for the Giants. "We knew the Dodgers had sent him to the minors. Then it leaked out, and a week in advance we started getting calls from the Japanese media, asking for press credentials. We issued 150 additional press passes that night."

The American press was there too. As Nomo worked his Tornado magic, they observed a feature that would become part of his trademark: At the end of each inning, as he stepped off the mound and headed back toward the dugout, Nomo tipped his hat to the fans. The gesture was a friendly acknowledgment, a way of thanking the crowd for their presence at the game. It was just what major league baseball needed— fan appreciation.

Before the game, Okumura had positioned himself behind the Dodgers' dugout—nonbaseball personnel were not allowed inside. Between innings he interpreted for Wallace and Nomo. Moorehead recalls that "in the first inning, after striking out Darren Lewis to start the inning, Nomo then walked the bases loaded." Wallace, sensing that Nomo was nervous, walked out to the mound. *"Hikuku"* the pitching coach told Nomo, "Keep the ball down." Soon after Wallace returned to the bench, Nomo got out of the inning by striking out Royce Clayton. No runs had scored. "The game went fifteen innings," Moorehead continues. "The Dodgers scored three in the top of the fifteenth, and we [the

Giants] came back with four to win in the bottom of the inning. It was an incredible game."

Nomo worked the first five innings. He allowed no runs and only one hit. He struck out seven and walked four. Each time Nomo struck out a batter, a fan would raise a large "K" card.

In the early innings when Nomo struck out a Giant, the only cheers were from his own dugout. But before long even Giants fans were cheering for Nomo. "I remember," says Moorehead, "that around the eighth inning the Japanese press started heading down to the press area for a postgame interview. I suppose they thought the game would end soon."

After the marathon game, Nomo told the press, "I'm so glad to pitch in a real major league game. This is what I always wanted. My dream is realized."

In Japan the event was front-page news. Sports papers made it their main story. The game was also broadcast live in Japan in the early hours of the morning (4:35 A.M.) via satellite by Japan's NHK television network. The Japanese media's take on the game could be summarized this way: A new era in baseball was dawning, and Nomo had made it happen. Almost overnight, Nomo went from traitor to an object of national pride. He was proving that Japanese players could play with the best. Rex Hudler, infielder with the California Angels, who played in Japan in 1993 for the Yakult Swallows, says of Nomo's performance: "That's no accident. He's schooled. He's got good stuff and he knows how to pitch. It's wonderful for baseball too. But it must have been hard for him (coming to the United States)," Hudler adds. "It's [Japan] a very closed society, and they don't like to let their athletes go."

Nomo's presence in the major leagues was indeed significant. Until the end of World War II in 1945, major league players were almost exclusively white. Not until the late 1940s with the arrival of Jackie Robinson, the major leagues' first African American player, did the sport finally break its color barrier. (Robinson also came up through the Dodger organization.) In the 1950s, Hispanic players from Cuba, the Dominican Republic, and Mexico entered the big leagues. These developments encouraged kids from minority groups across the country that they, too, might one day have a shot at playing in the pros. And although Asians had never been openly excluded from major league baseball, precious few had been able to break into the big leagues. Nomo was one of those few.

Nomo's first game in the majors was followed by a bruising administered in Denver by the Colorado Rockies on May 7. In a game the Dodgers eventually won 12 to 10, Nomo allowed seven earned runs. He earned a no-decision for the game. His performance was a definite disappointment, and Japanese and American fans began to wonder if the Tornado could compete in the big leagues. This game was followed by another no-decision start against the St. Louis Cardinals in Los Angeles on May 12. The Tornado was in something of a rut.

Then came a taste of the season to follow. In another no-decision game against Pittsburgh at Dodger stadium on May 17, the rookie struck out fourteen Pirates. Throughout the game the crowd often gave Nomo a standing ovation when he struck out a batter. At other points they chanted his name—"Noooo-Mowww. Nooo-Mowww." After the game, Tom Candiotti, a veteran pitcher in the Dodgers' rotation, commented on Nomo. "He goes about his work real professionally, and in the process, I think he's earned everyone's respect around here."

Dodger manager Tommy Lasorda, who was in his nineteenth year coaching the club, witnessed the daily pressure Nomo was under from the Japanese press. "They want to know everything he eats. They watch every move he makes. They want to know everything I tell him. They asked me, 'What are you going to tell him tomorrow?' I said, 'I don't know, I'll wait until tomorrow.'"

Two different sources of pressure were building up against the Tornado: the crush of the press, and the desire to win his first game. After yet another well-pitched no-decision at New York, Nomo lost 5 to 1 to the Montreal Expos on May 28. He allowed only three runs, striking out seven, but he was wild. He walked seven batters.

Nomo began to take exception to some of the stories that were appearing about him in the Japanese papers. According to Okumura, a cover story bylined by Masanori Murakami appeared in *Weekly Baseball,* a tabloid newspaper widely distributed throughout Japan. In the piece, Murakami offered advice to Nomo about how to succeed in the major leagues. Nomo was not pleased.

Despite the string of no-decisions and Nomo's losing record, fans were showing up at the game with placards and signs bearing greetings in Japanese. Stadiums across the country were welcoming new fans because of Nomo's appeal. And as Nomo began to travel around the National League, his press following continued to grow. Thus, with the acceptance of a Japanese player in American baseball, the game truly started to become a more international sport. And Nomo hadn't even won a game yet.

A delighted Hideo Nomo displays his new Los Angeles Dodger jersey.

Surrounded by (from left) Fred Claire, Charlie Blaney, and Peter O'Malley, Nomo signs contract to play in the Dodger organization.

Dodger President Peter O'Malley shakes hands with Nomo and Korean teammate Chan Ho Park.

The Tornado's legs and hips power his delivery to the plate.

A group of cheerleaders lead the crowd in song at a ballpark in Japan.

Nomo fans unfurl a banner of the Japanese flag at Dodger Stadium.

Nomo shares a laugh in the dugout with pitcher, teammate, and friend Ismael Valdes.

Former Dodger star and 1981 National League Rookie of the Year Fernando Valenzuela poses with Nomo.

In Japan, Shinto priests bless a baseball field on opening day.

CHAPTER 7

SIX NIGHTS OF NOMOMANIA

On June 2, 1995, Hideo Nomo won his first game in the major leagues. It would be the first in a streak that would bring him to the attention of American baseball fans and spur *Los Angeles Times* sports columnist Mike Downey to coin a new word—"Nomomania."

Before 31,002 curious fans at Dodger Stadium, Nomo struck out six in eight innings and scored a 2 to 1 victory over the New York Mets. After the game, Dodger first baseman Eric Karros presented Nomo with the game ball. In the Dodger clubhouse, Nomo could be seen with champagne bottle in hand, celebrating. "I'm very, very happy and very glad," Nomo said through his interpreter Michael Okumura. Nomo's record was now one win, one loss, with 55 strikeouts, the second highest number of K's in the National League.

After the game, Nomo made a call back to Japan. "He called me after his first win," remembers his father. "He was very happy."

His next start on the Dodger homestand was also a win. On June 7, Nomo beat the Montreal Expos 7 to 1. He went eight innings and struck out four.

The following day the phones rang off the hook in the downtown Los Angeles office of Japan Travel Bureau (JTB), Japan's largest travel agency. Japanese baseball fans and Nomo admirers were calling the L.A. agency to book a trip to Southern California. They wanted to come to L.A. to see Nomo pitch.

According to Howard Burk, who handled many of the Nomo calls, "As soon as the Dodgers signed Nomo, the calls started coming in. One time we had a group of Japanese tourists in town who were not scheduled to go to a game, but so many requested to see Nomo, we wound up taking a group of 500 to Dodger Stadium. From then on we didn't even have to promote it." The three-day JTB tour came to include airfare, hotel accommodations, meals, and a seat to see Nomo pitch. The price for the package deal started at $1,300 and rose to $2,600. As Nomo began to win more and more games and his fame grew, the action at JTB "became bigger than life," Burk says. "It got to be strange. People who knew little about baseball were suddenly interested. We would get calls from people in Japan who said, 'I am going to be in Los Angeles on such and such a date, could you have Nomo pitch on that day?' We have even gotten calls requesting Nomo's '96 pitching schedule—as if we knew!"

Many tourists also requested to be taken to Paul's Kitchen, a Chinese restaurant open in Los Angeles since 1944. While dining at Paul's Kitchen, Japanese fans enjoy looking at the wall covered with Dodger photos, which includes a photo of Hideo Nomo. The menu even includes a Tommy Lasorda Special. According to Ken Ng, a host at Paul's, the special is also Nomo's favorite.

Hungry? Ready for a true Dodger meal? The Tommy Lasorda Special at Paul's Kitchen in Los Angeles is quite a feast. It includes:

Wonton Soup
Egg Rolls
Barbecue Pork
Spareribs
Asparagus Beef
Fried Rice
Shrimp in Lobster Sauce
Chicken with Vegetables
Sweet and Sour Shrimp

Full yet?

As the season progressed, the Tornado continued his destructive path through National League hitters. On June 14, the Tornado blew through Pittsburgh and into the record books. Nomo tied a Dodger rookie mark of sixteen strikeouts. He went eight innings, allowing only two earned runs in the Dodgers' 8 to 5 win over the Pirates. "Everything he does makes you look ugly," Pirate left fielder Al Martin remarked after the game. "This guy paints the corners as good as anyone in the game," added Pirate catcher Mark Parent. "And his forkball is the best in the game."

In St. Louis on June 19, Nomo registered another win, 5 to 2, and struck out eight to run his total to eighty-three for the still-young season. This was followed by his fifth win in the streak, a gem he threw against San Francisco. Nomo struck out thirteen San Francisco Giants in a 7 to 0 shutout. And if the rookie pitcher had strolled through downtown San Francisco after the game, he would have seen his likeness on T-shirts and jackets in the windows of sporting good stores. Nomomania had now arrived in Northern California.

The Dodgers returned home on June 29. Their first game of the homestand drew 46,295, all wanting to see Nomo. The Dodgers' press office issued 131 press passes—seventy-five to Japanese correspondents. The walk-up ticket line stretched almost to the parking lot. The Dodgers were hosting the Colorado Rockies. Although the season had not yet reached its halfway point, it was clear that the Dodgers and the Rockies would fight for the top spot in the National League's Western division. Nomo plus the Rockies—the game had special appeal.

After the last pitch was thrown, Nomo had struck out thirteen of the hard-hitting Rockies in a 3 to 0 complete-game shutout. The win put the Dodgers in first place, a half game over the Rockies.

Not known for staying until the end of games, Dodger fans sat in their seats until the last pitch, watching Nomo strike out Walt Weiss for his fiftieth strikeout in four games. With that K, Nomo broke a record of forty-nine strikeouts in four games held by Dodger great pitcher Sandy Koufax. "I'm very honored to be compared to Koufax," Nomo commented after the game.

During that homestand, it became clear that Nomo was developing stronger ties to his fellow teammates. He and Mike Piazza, the team's All-Star catcher, were communicating perfectly well about balls, strikes, fastballs, and forkballs.

Nomo also was developing a close friendship with another Dodger—pitcher Ismael Valdes. These two shared a common bond. Each had recently come to America and neither spoke English. "They always sat next to each other in the dugout," pitching coach Dave Wallace says. "And during the games, Nomo learned some Spanish, and Valdes some Japanese." Wallace feels that throughout the season the two pitchers picked each other up, helping the Dodger team spirit.

During the Tornado's six-game winning streak, the words *Hideo Nomo* became music to one man's ears. He was Southern California songwriter Stan Esecson. Stan had recently read an article about the earthquake disaster in Kobe, Japan. He had been hearing a lot about Nomo, too. Then one day Stan had a brainstorm. He wanted to do something to help the earthquake victims. "I was eating lunch with my son Sammy, and I started writing down lyrics on a napkin." He then attached the words to the tune of the well-known "Banana Boat" song.

The first verse of the song goes:

"Hey, Mr. Dodgerman, thanks for signing Nomo,
The whole world's watching Nomomania."

After producing and publishing the song, Esecson made calls to the American Red Cross, and in a few weeks he set up a deal giving the organization a portion of the profits. The money will be used to help the victims of the Kobe quake as well as those in need in Southern California.

And Nomomania went beyond songs. It also became part of the international computer network called the Internet. The Worldwide Web (WWW) is part of the Internet. The Web is organized into "pages" of pictures and text on specific subjects. It reaches millions of computer users around the world. A Japanese computer expert and Nomo fan named Koichi Ono had created a web site (a series of web pages) on the Internet called the Tornado Boy Home Page. David Morris, an informal reporter for the page who lives in Orange County,

Wondering how the rest of that famous Nomo song goes? Well, here goes:

Verse 2
He throw 6K, 7K, 8K bunch,
When Nomo pitch they eat their lunch.
He throws the forkball and it zing right by,
The next thing you know the ump says goodbye.

Chorus
Everybody
Day-o, Heday-ay-ay-o
He-day-oh Nomo true Dodger Blue

Verse 3
They call him Tornado 'cus of how he spin,
Nomo pitch, the Dodgers win.
He's got great stuff and deceptive motion,
He came across the Pacific Ocean.

California, says, "Many of us who contribute to the page are all baseball fans who've found something personal in Nomo's achievement." On the site there are pictures of Nomo, recaps of games from Tornado Boy Home Page reporters around the country, as well as a place to leave messages and exchange e-mail—all about Nomo.

As the All-Star break approached, baseball card dealers and brokers of signed Nomo goods reported a surge in interest and sales. Robert Klevin, vice president of Sports Card Heaven Inc., in Davie, Florida, reports receiving calls from "Hawaii, Texas, Alaska—all over the country!" for Japanese Nomo baseball cards.

Robin Otani, owner of Jam and Hoopla, a card and collectible shop in Torrance, California, also reported strong sales for Nomo items. "We sold signed jerseys and autographed Nomo balls." Otani actually reported selling a pair of shoes that Nomo wore in a game for $1,000.

"Being Japanese, I'm very proud of him," says Otani. "This year he saved the major leagues and helped my business, too." Jaime Jarrin, a Dodger broadcaster and former interpreter for Fernando Valenzuela says, "I thought I'd never see anything like Fernandomania again in my life. It's bringing back very sweet memories of 1981."

After the Colorado game, a jubilant Tommy Lasorda declared, "Everybody loves Nomo. The Japanese community. Americans. Baseball. Nomomania is here."

Hideo Nomo had an awesome June 1995. He won six games and lost none with an ERA of 0.89. That means he gave up less than one earned run every nine innings. By July 1, the Tornado had helped the Dodgers climb into first place in the National League West. The fans were happy. Tommy Lasorda was happy. The twenty-six-year-old rookie pitcher from Japan was happy. And Nomomania was sweeping the country.

CHAPTER 8

PENNANT FEVER

The All-Star game was less than two weeks away.

June had brought Nomo to the attention of fans, major leaguers, and coaches. After his six-game winning streak, Nomo's record was six and one, with an ERA of 2.05. And if that was not enough, the rookie led the National League in strikeouts with 109.

Nomo became the first Japanese player to be named to the All-Star squad. That wasn't all. A few days before the game, Atlanta Braves' star and starting All-Star pitcher Greg Maddux announced that he could not play due to a sore pitching hand. Nomo was then penciled in as the starter. He would not only be the first Japanese player ever to play in the All-Star game—now *he* would be the starter.

The Sixty-Sixth Annual Major League All-Star Game

was a night of wonders. The Ballpark in Arlington, home of the Texas Rangers, was a wonder in itself, complete with a Legends of the Game Baseball Museum, a Walk of Fame, and murals of Babe Ruth, Ty Cobb, Willie Mays, and other baseball legends.

The day of the game, Nomo arrived at the ballpark early. This was going to be an event to remember, and he was not going to miss a minute of it. His wife and son had come all the way from Japan for the occasion. It was a very special night. Before the game began, he came out on the field in street clothes to do interviews for Japanese television.

Nomo's National League team failed to score in the top of the first. Nomo took the mound in the bottom of the inning. He allowed a single to Carlos Baerga (who was thrown out trying to steal second by catcher Mike Piazza), but struck out both Kenny Lofton and Edgar Martinez to end the inning.

In the second inning, Nomo first got Frank "the Big Hurt" Thomas to foul out. Then he faced the fiercest power hitter in the major leagues, Albert Belle, who would hit fifty home runs that season. Nomo struck him out. His last test was Cal Ripken, Jr., who was well on his way to breaking Lou Gherig's record for most consecutive games played. He lined out to right field. Nomo's All-Star totals were one hit, zero runs, zero bases on balls, and three strikeouts. Not bad for a kid with a funny windup and an Industrial League forkball.

"After the All-Star Game, there was a big increase in mail," Nomo's interpreter Michael Okumura said. "We received forty to fifty letters per day. Mail over the season ran about 70 percent from the United States and 30 percent from Japan."

In the opening days of July, after the All-Star break, the Dodgers trailed the division-leading Rockies by four games. No one had taken the Rockies seriously, but their mile-high hitters, Andres Gallaraga, Dante Bichete, and Larry Walker, could quickly wipe the smile from any pitcher's face. If the Dodgers were to catch the Rockies, their pitching rotation of Ramon Martinez, Ismael Valdes, Tom Candiotti, and Hideo Nomo would need to come through.

Nomo's first start after the All-Star break was memorable. It was July 15 at Dodger Stadium. Ramon Martinez had pitched a no-hitter the night before against the Florida Marlins. Would there be two no-hitters in a row? The Marlins broke up that talk with a hit in the second inning. But Nomo went on to strike out ten in a 3 to 1 win before 45,499 fans. In that game, Nomo earned his first major league hit in thirty-two at bats. He singled off Bobby Witt in the seventh inning. Nomo's record was seven and one, but the Dodgers still trailed the Rockies by four and a half games.

Nomo got his next win against the Central Division-leading Cincinnati Reds on July 30. The Reds were a pitcher's nightmare, fast, powerful, and smart. But

What else do Nomo's new and old homes have in common? Like Los Angeles, Kobe, Japan also experienced a recent major earthquake. Their quake, however, came one year after the 6.5 quake in Los Angeles, on January 17, 1995. The intense shaking in Kobe lasted about twenty seconds and measured 7.2 on Japan's Richter scale and 6.8 on the American Richter scale. More than 5,000 people died from the Japanese quake, which caused more than $99 billion in property damage.

Nomo beat them 5 to 4, going eight innings and striking out eleven. Unfortunately, Colorado kept winning, and the Dodgers trailed the Rockies by five games.

Throughout the summer, fans continued to come out to the ballpark in big numbers to see Nomo pitch. On nights the Tornado took the mound, the Dodgers sold 5,000 more tickets per game than when the other Dodger starters pitched. On the road, he was responsible for similar attendance increases.

In early August, Nomo and the Dodgers headed back to San Francisco for a rematch against their long-time West Coast rivals. By coincidence, August 5 had been scheduled to be a night of tribute for Masanori Murakami, the first Japanese to play in the major leagues. It was Murakami's night, but it was Nomo's game. Before a packed Candlestick Park crowd and a large television audience, the Tornado pitched his best game of the year—a one-hitter. He went the distance, striking out eleven in a 3 to 0 win. Better yet, the Dodgers were gaining on Colorado, now only three and a half games back.

In the middle of August, the Rockies went into a slide. The Dodgers steadily gained ground, and on August 13, they took sole possession of first place.

On August 15, Nomomania was in full bloom at Dodger Stadium. Forty-eight thousand fans came out to the ballpark that night to see Nomo pitch against the Cubs. For Dodger fans, it was a familiar, yet somehow foreign, experience. Sushi was being sold at concession stands; the Japanese fast-food company Yoshinoya was selling beef and rice to both Asian and non-Asian fans. People ate with chopsticks as they watched the game. Longtime Dodger announcer Vin Scully started counting off Nomo's strikeouts in Japanese . . . *ichi, ni, san, shi,* etc. More than 2,000 Japanese tourists were in attendance. On the stadium's concourse level, a young woman armed with a Japanese/English dictionary answered inquiries about season tickets. Japanese TV crews busied themselves doing interviews with radiant fans who left the souvenir stands with treasured armloads of Nomo T-shirts.

Then there was the game. And what a game. It was one of Nomo's more gutsy performances even though it started poorly. Nomo gave up three runs in the first inning. Then, in the fourth, Cub pitcher Steve Trachsel loaded the bases for 1994 Rookie of the Year right fielder Raul Mondesi. Bam—a grand slam put the Dodgers ahead 4 to 3. Nomo, who would speak later of having a sore elbow, only went six innings. But the Dodgers went on to win 7 to 4, extending their lead over the Rockies to two and a half games.

Inning after inning of that crucial game, Nomo would get in a jam—and then get out of trouble by using his forkball. It was the same pitching strategy he used much of the summer. He set the batters up with a quick strike—fastball, then a wicked forkball almost in the dirt, then either outside or inside. If the batter fouled off a fastball or two, he would finish him with a forkball that dropped just a heartbeat before it crossed the plate. "His forkball tumbles and has a very late break," says Dave Wallace, the Dodgers' pitching coach.

Dodger fans were really beginning to show enthusiasm for this team. "They helped the image of L.A," said Howard Burk, a representative of the Japan Travel Bureau. "Every year in L.A. it was something else—fire, floods, riots. Nomo and the Dodgers brought tourists to L.A. who would never have come here previously."

Still, there were forty-two games left to play. Could the Dodgers hold off Colorado?

Nomo's next start was on the road against the New York Mets on August 20. Even though supportive fans greeted him there with colorful Japanese carp kites, he lost the game 5 to 3. It wasn't all bad, though. He did strike out thirteen Mets. After that August game, his record was ten wins and four losses with 188 strike-outs.

In Nomo's next start on August 25, he was bombed by Philadelphia. He gave up seven runs on six hits—in only three innings. Baseball writers and Nomo's team-mates began to wonder if the fans and especially the media were beginning to affect his pitching. Sometimes reporters and camera crews would huddle around Nomo just minutes before he went to the mound.

Dodger manager Tommy Lasorda decided to take action. "We're hoping to try to minimize all this and try to keep everyone away from him," he said. "Nomo just wants to pitch against major leaguers," Nomo's inter-preter Michael Okumura says. "Nomo is not interested in being a celebrity or a hero. But people treat him as a hero."

Despite their loss, the Dodgers still maintained their Western Division lead—but only by a half-game. They would need Nomo's full concentration to win the title.

On August 31, the Mets had Nomo's complete atten-tion. That night was his twenty-seventh birthday, and he had good reason to celebrate. He went seven-plus innings in a 6 to 5 Dodger win. Relief pitcher Tod Worrell got the win, but Nomo pitched well.

Dave Morris, of the Tornado Boy Home Page, was there. It was Nomo's birthday and Morris remembers seeing fans holding up Japanese-language signs that read, "Happy Birthday, Nomo."

"They had downloaded the message from the Web site," Morris said. And a happy day it was. With that win the Dodgers remained in first by a full game.

Nomo missed his next start. The nail on his middle finger had cracked, and it hurt when he pitched. A manicurist placed an acrylic wrap on the broken nail to keep it in place. When asked about the crack, Coach Wallace responded, "Nomo told me the fingernail problems are from throwing the fastball. The seams (where he grips the ball) are higher on the ball here than in Japan."

On September 5, his new nail intact, Nomo got another shot at Philadelphia—the team that had blown him out earlier in the season. This time he was the master, striking out seven. Some of these seven were the same players who had crushed him in the last game. Commenting on this reversal of fortune, Coach Wallace said, "Baseball is a constant game of adjustment. Nomo remembers the games. How he got certain hitters out . . . he studies the hitters—he studies their weaknesses." Relief pitcher Cummings got the 2 to 1 win, keeping the Dodgers one game up in the division.

The next two weeks, the Dodgers went into a slide.

The pitching was good enough, but their hitting had gone far south. Nomo won a game in Chicago and lost one at home on August 19 to San Francisco. The Dodgers were now in second place, a game and a half back to the surging Rockies.

But if the Rockies were going to win the division, they would have to beat the Dodgers at home. The stage was set for real baseball drama. A showdown series between the Rockies and the Dodgers would decide the pennant. If the Rockies won all three games, it was over. They came into Dodger Stadium thinking *sweep*. They didn't get it. Nomo didn't pitch, but the Dodgers took two

Nomo's financial impact on the game of baseball goes way beyond a boost in Dodger ticket sales. According to Tim Brosnan, who works in the international sales department for the National League, Nomo has broadened interest in American baseball around the world. Requests for National League broadcasts have increased in Japan, Taiwan, and South Korea, just to name a few places.

out of three games to squeeze a half-game up in the standings.

Now all the Dodgers had to do was beat the Padres, in San Diego. For the Dodgers, Jack Murphy Stadium in San Diego was the home of the "Dodger Black and Blue." That's how poorly they played there over the years. But they had to finish their season in San Diego. It was a three-game series, and the Dodgers could clinch at least a tie for the division title by winning the first game. They lost.

The next start fell to Nomo. In his previous start he had beaten the Padres at Dodger Stadium. Now he looked tired and worn thin, and this time he was facing the Padres on their own playground. But Colorado had lost the night before, and now the Dodgers could clinch the division with one win.

The Dodgers jumped ahead from the start and never let the Padres catch up. It was a crucial game and Nomo pitched eight brilliant, pressure-packed innings to clinch the pennant for the Dodgers.

The baseball stories that his father told Hideo Nomo as a child were coming true—the classic matchups of strength against strength. He'd come such a long way from playing catch in the park with his father.

Since then, those childhood tosses had gained adult strength and velocity. The boy from Osaka had grown and watched and learned to deal with the hard days that baseball gives to every player. He'd taken a great voyage, traveled across the Pacific Ocean in hopes of finding a new home to play ball. He'd played well. He'd met friends in a new country. And now he'd won the most important game of the 1995 regular season. The Tornado had stormed through San Diego, striking out eleven batters and clinching the Western Division title for his team.

Back in Osaka, Japan, Nomo's father leaned closer to the TV set. He watched his son and the other Dodger players gather on the infield at Jack Murphy Stadium to congratulate one another. Never before had he seen such a smile on his son's face.

POSTSEASON

After winning the Western Division, the Dodgers had to face the slick-fielding, good-hitting Cincinnati Reds. The Reds had run away with the Central Division title early in the season. The Dodgers had to beat them to have a shot at the National League pennant. It didn't go well for Nomo and the Dodgers. They quickly lost the first two games in the five-game Division Series. Nomo started game three. That evening he didn't have his best stuff. He allowed a two-run homer to Ron Gant in the first, and a one-run shot to Bret Boone in the third. He then struggled through two more scoreless innings. In the sixth, he allowed two singles, threw one wild pitch, and finally was taken out of the game. Though he pitched with a lot of heart and determination and even struck out six batters, the Dodgers could not pull out a win. They eventually lost the game (10 to 1) and the series.

After sweeping the Dodgers, the Reds played the Atlanta Braves for the National League pennant. They were swept four games to none. The Braves beat the Cleveland Indians four games to two to win the World Series.

On November 9, 1995, the news all Nomo fans around the world had been hoping and waiting for was announced: Hideo Nomo was named the National League Rookie of the Year for 1995. He was the first Japanese-born player to earn this postseason honor. In the balloting, Nomo received 118 of the Baseball Writers Association of America votes. The runner-up, Atlanta Braves third baseman Chipper Jones, received 104 votes.

Though Nomo was not a rookie to the professional baseball scene, he was a trail-blazing rookie in major league baseball. He finished the season 13 and 6 with an ERA of 2.54. He struck out a total of 236 batters in 191⅓ innings to lead the National League. It was the fourth consecutive season a Los Angeles Dodger won Rookie of the Year. In 1995, Hideo Nomo joined the ranks of teammates Eric Karros, Mike Piazza, and Raul Mondesi as a recipient of the prestigious award.

In 1995, Hideo Nomo ranked among the National League's Top 10 in six pitching categories:

EARNED RUN AVERAGE

1.63	Maddux	ATL
2.54	*Nomo*	*L.A.*
2.94	Ashby	S.D.
3.05	Valdes	L.A.
3.08	Glavine	ATL
3.08	Hamilton	S.D.

COMPLETE GAMES

10	Maddux	ATL
7	Leiter	S.F.
6	Valdes	L.A.
5	Neagle	PGH
4	*Nomo*	*L.A.*
4	Martinez	L.A.

WINS

19	Maddux	ATL
18	Schourek	CIN
17	Martinez	L.A.
16	Glavine	ATL
14	Rapp	FLA
14	Martinez	MTL
14	Navarro	CHI
14	Burkett	FLA
13	*Nomo*	*L.A.*
13	(3 others tied)	

OPPONENTS BATTING AVG.

.182	*Nomo*	*L.A.*
.197	Maddux	ATL
.227	Martinez	MTL

WINNING PCT.

.905	Maddux	ATL
.720	Schourek	CIN
.714	Burba	CIN
.708	Martinez	L.A.
.706	Smiley	CIN
.700	Navarro	CHI
.696	Glavine	ATL
.684	*Nomo*	*L.A.*

SHUTOUTS

3	*Nomo*	*L.A.*
3	Maddux	ATL
2	(10 players tied)	

Glossary

ARCHIPELAGO—a chain of islands

BALL—a ball that is thrown outside the strike zone

BASE ON BALLS—(or walk)—an advance to first base awarded to a batter who is pitched four balls during one at bat

CALLIGRAPHY—artistic or stylized handwriting

CAMPO LAS PALMAS—Dominican Republic baseball facility founded by Dodger owner Peter O'Malley to help develop the talents of Domincan ballplayers

CHIBA (Chee-bah) LOTTE MARINES—Japanese professional baseball team

CY YOUNG AWARD—major league baseball's award for the best pitcher of the baseball season

DAIEI HAWKS—Japanese professional baseball team

DODGERTOWN—home of Los Angeles Dodgers' spring training facility in Vero Beach, Florida

EMPEROR HIROHITO—Japanese emperor from 1926 to 1989

ERA—(earned run average) formula used to calculate the number of runs per inning allowed by a pitcher, not including runners allowed on base by errors or allowed a chance to bat because of an error

FASTBALL—pitch thrown at full speed, sometimes reaching 100 miles per hour

FORKBALL—a deceptive fast pitch that suddenly drops or darts as it approaches the batter

HANSHIN (hahn-sheen) TIGERS—Osaka-based Japanese professional baseball team

HIKUKU (hee-koo-koo)—Japanese word meaning "low" or "down"

HONSHU (hohn-shoo)—largest island in the Japanese archipelago

ICHI, NI, SAN, SHI, . . . (ee-chee, nee, sahn, shee)—Japanese for one, two, three, four

INDUSTRIAL LEAGUE—Japan's amateur baseball league

INTERNET—a network that connects computer users throughout the world

"K"—letter often held up by fans at ball games to indicate a strikeout; an abbreviation for strikeout on a scorecard

KANJI—a character in the Japanese writing system

KARAOKE (kah-rah-oh-keh)—a form of entertainment in which people sing to previously recorded instrumental music

KI (kee)—Japanese word that can mean spirit or tree, among other things

KINTETSU (keen-tets-oo) RAILWAY COMPANY—Japanese railroad company for which the Kintetsu Buffaloes baseball team is named

KINTETSU BUFFALOES—Japanese professional baseball team

KOBE (koh-beh)—Japanese city that was devastated by an earthquake on January 17, 1995

KONOHANA-KU (koh-noh-hah-nah-koo)—district in Osaka, where Nomo was born

KOSHIEN (koh-shee-ehn) STADIUM—Japanese baseball stadium; site of the National High School Championship tournament

MINATO-KU (mee-nah-toh-koo)—district in Osaka, Japan, near Konohana-ku (Nomo's birthplace)

SAKANA (sah-kah-nah)—Japanese word for fish

SEWAMURA (say-wah-moo-rah)—Japanese equivalent of the Cy Young Award

SHIN-NITTETSU SAKAI (sheen-nee-tets-oo sah-keye)—Osaka-based Industrial League baseball team

SHUTOUT—pitching performance in which a pitcher allows no runs in game

STRIKE—a pitched ball that passes through the strike zone, is swung on and missed, or fouled away

STRIKE ZONE—the area over home plate through which the baseball must be thrown in order to be called a strike

SUMO (soo-moh) WRESTLING—a form of wrestling popular in Japan

SUSHI (soo-shee)—Japanese cuisine; sliced fish, often raw, vegetable, or egg on vinegared rice

UDON (oo-dohn)—Japanese cuisine; thick noodles marinated in soy paste

UNAGI (oo-nah-gee)—Japanese word for eel

WALK—*see* Base on Balls

WORLD SERIES—major league baseball's championship series

WORLD WIDE WEB—a part of the Internet computer network

YAKITORI (yah-kee-toh-ree)—Japanese cuisine; grilled chicken on a skewer

YAKULT SWALLOWS—Tokyo-based Japanese professional baseball team

YOKOHAMA (yoh-koh-hah-mah) BAYSTARS—Japanese professional baseball team

YOKOHAMA STADIUM—small Japanese baseball stadium, home to the Yokohama Baystars

YOMIURI (yoh-mee-oo-ree) GIANTS—Tokyo-based Japanese professional baseball team

INDEX

ABOUT THE AUTHOR

Edmon J. Rodman is a writer and designer of children's books who lives with his wife and three children in Los Angeles, California. *Nomo: The Tornado Who Took America by Storm* is his fourth book.